Atheism

নাস্তিকতা

NK Mondal

ISBN 978-93-5458-715-3

Published in India 2021 by Pencil

A brand of

One Point Six Technologies Pvt. Ltd.

123, Building J2, Shram Seva Premises,

Wadala Truck Terminal, Wadala (E)

Mumbai 400037, Maharashtra, INDIA

E connect@thepencilapp.com

W www.thepencilapp.com

Author biography

NK Mondal is an Indian poet, social consultant, social and humanitarian activist, humanist, columnist, novelist, philosopher and writer. He was born in 1997 in the village of Pratappur in the Hariharpara block of Murshidabad district in the Indian state of West Bengal to a poor Muslim family. Although his birth name is Selim Sheikh, he is better known in the world as NK Mondal. In 2019, he was awarded the title of Sahitya Ratna. Father Saiful Sheikh and mother Menuka Bibi. Although the beloved writer had a good education, he had to face ridicule, slander, oppression and even death threats from various religious people. He has set an example in the area as a very honest and just person from a young age, yet he is humiliated by the pious. Because the author is a true Islamic, Despite repeated threats to speak out against misconceptions and violent laws, he continues to write with courage. Although he is a writer, he is actually a philosopher and has many talents. Although he is Islamic, he continues to write about theism, atheism, religion, society, country, movement, free thought, etc. Notable books are Love, The Ideal Human, Misconceptions and Orthodoxy, Beautiful Daughters, etc.

CONTENTS

Atheism

Atheism

The real meaning of the word religion is to contain On the other hand, it is said that the characteristics of living beings and objects But all the traditional religions that the common people follow are called religions These religions are generally practiced by 99.9% of the people, which still exist on earth There are approximately five and a half thousand religions in the world, such as Christianity, Buddhism, Sikhism, Persian,

Christianity, etc. Islam is the latest and final religion in the mouths of Islamic scholars But lately, a new religion has emerged in the developed world, the Americas The name of the religion is Satanic religion Which was founded by Lucien Graves and one of his co-workers, The last religion like the account is now the Satanic Temple People on earth have not chosen one or two religions About five and a half thousand religions have come into the world But did people really need so much religion? And why or one by one different guides Why is it that there are different opinions? Some people support idolatry and some do not Many say that their religion is sent by God This is what the followers of almost all religions say Then the rest of the religions are not sent by God If all religions are sent by God, then why there is no resemblance of any religion with any other religion There may be some similarities, such as policy words, but they are also said by wise people And why are different religions sent by the same God? He could send religion at once And he could instruct all the wise men he sent to preach the same principle And if God is omnipotent, If everything happens in His will, not even a leaf of a tree moves without His will, then why did God Almighty send guides without doing anything? He was the one who could show the way to the people What God wants, there is no God at all

| | Two | |

The first thing we need to know is that in today's age of well-educated civilized modern science, all the prevailing social group religions are, in my opinion, "religion is only a fictional form and belief". Which in reality is not even seen in the drops People generally believe that there is a God He is the One who created and will destroy And He will resurrect all, and they will be called to account He is the one who sent different sages or guides for different communities in different eras. So did different communities have different importance and dignity to God? And if he were an equal judge, why did he send a guide for different communities, for all the people of the world? He did not do that, just the opposite Sent a lot of guides to the world, did you really need so many guides, He is the Almighty, He can do everything, so why did He send so many guides? He is the one who manages everything, he couldn't do this little thing, he needed a guide. Where in the world there is no need for a guide to guide anyone but man, he is the one who handles everything. But why did wise people need a guide? The knowledge of other living beings is not accessible. Usually they needed a guide, but they did not give them to humans. And if the guides of all religions were sent by God, then why were they divided and their followers still follow different laws? The same law could be, And all those guides could preach the same principle But no one did Each guide had a different policy If they had been sent by God, they would have preached differently instead of preaching one principle So did God have different dignity for different people? Nor did God love people of any age and did not love anyone God is not a hypocrite, nor are God's guides hypocrites Otherwise God has said one thing and they have done another Nor does God sometimes change laws like humans And if that was not the case, then different scholars would have been sent at different times to preach different laws to the people Or the same principle could be preached by all scholars And if a law is against God, why don't you ban guides? Why Moses for the Jewish nation, Jesus for the Christian nation No, the guides sent by God are hypocrites Otherwise God has said one thing and they have done another Nor does God sometimes change laws like humans And if that was not the case, then different scholars would have been sent at different times to preach different laws to the people Or the same principle could be preached by all scholars And if a law is against God, why don't you ban guides? Why Moses for the Jewish nation, Jesus for the Christian nation No, the guides sent by God are hypocrites Otherwise God has said one thing and they have done another Nor does God sometimes change laws like humans And if that were not the case, then different scholars would have been sent at different times to preach different laws to the people Or the same principle could be preached by all scholars And if a law is against God, why don't you ban guides? Moses for the Jewish nation, Jesus for the Christian nation

(Question subject)

What is the right religion? And which is the right religion?

First of all, it has been said that the real meaning of the word religion is to contain and refer to the qualities or characteristics of living beings and objects That is, the quality of human life is the real religion of human life And for all these, wise men and wise men are born Usually those different thinkers had different views and ideals And we followed them, which we still follow the different views and ideals of wise people But in the true sense of the word, the apostles were supposed to be one and the same, but that never happened. Religion is basically the good deeds of human life This is exactly how many wise men were born in the world But I don't think they are sent by God Tinara was a man of good deeds, morals, skillful knowledge, free from prejudices, compassionate man, afflicted with pain, a believer in God, a theist, a social reformer, a non-violent person. And saw and understood and accepted the ideals and principles of the three People used to follow them, which is still being practiced as a religion Yes it is true, I have to admit that if the name of adhering to those principles or ideals is religion then I accept it as religion. Of all the religions and philosophers that have come into the world, whether God has sent them or not, some religions are at least better for me, such as Islam (Hazrat Muhammad SAW), Christianity (Jesus Christ or Jesus AS), Judaism (Moses AS). However, these are also considered to be part of the religion of Islam, as evidenced by various texts Among these three religions, there are beautiful and best principles and ideals in Islam The law of Islam is basically humanistic and useful to all and scientific If religion is the name of adhering to those principles or ideals, then I accept it as religion Of all the religions and philosophers that have come into the world, whether God has sent them or not, some religions are at least better for me, such as Islam (Hazrat Muhammad SAW), Christianity (Jesus Christ or Jesus AS), Judaism (Moses AS). However, these are also considered to be part of Islam, as evidenced by various texts Among these three religions, there are beautiful and best principles and ideals in Islam The law of Islam is basically humanistic and useful to all and scientific If religion is the name of adhering to those principles or ideals, then I accept it as religion Of all the religions and philosophers that have come into the world, whether God has sent them or not, some religions are at least better for me, such as Islam (Hazrat Muhammad SAW), Christianity (Jesus Christ or Jesus AS), Judaism (Moses AS). However, these are also considered to be part of Islam, as evidenced by various texts Among these three religions, there are beautiful and best principles and ideals in Islam The law of Islam is basically humanistic and useful to all and scientific Evidence of which is also in various texts Among these three religions, there are beautiful and best principles and ideals in Islam The law of Islam is basically humanistic and useful to all and scientific Evidence of which is also in various texts Among these three religions, there are beautiful and best principles and ideals in

Islam The law of Islam is basically humanistic and useful to all and scientific

2) If God Himself is omnipotent, then why did He send guides and why did they need them?

It is said that God is one and unique This has been acknowledged in the texts of almost every religion In some religions, even though God is one, the worship of gods is done If they obey God, why do they worship the gods sent by God? He could worship the Almighty God It is accepted in every religion that it has sent guides through the ages No religion can deny it But here the question arises, if God is omnipotent, why did He send a human guide, He could do everything. But he did not do that and sent in the form of a human incarnation He gives rain, he gives sunshine, he can do everything In some religions he has created the jinn and the human race in the best way He did not send a guide for the jinn nation from age to age, but why did he lead for the human race. But mankind is the best and wisest of all, But why did he send a guide for those wise men? Genes and different species of creatures could or would send for them But why did He send a guide for those who walk with wisdom and conscience? It is said and recorded that angels or messengers would bring God's message to the guides, but what was the need for these angels, why not God Himself could send the message directly to the guide. But God did not do that God could manage food, clothing, space, everything for everyone from that invisible place, but he could not guide the human race. But he did not send a guide, but why Can't God bring mankind under his control? When he had everything under control, he could do that, But he did not do this and sent a guide Even after sending so many guides, they have not been able to control the human race. On the contrary, there are more people in the way of Satan, but why? Is Satan more powerful than God? No evil guide has come from the devil And if he also breeds, then he is as powerful as Satan's God. And if someone says that the devil cannot increase the lineage, then how did so many devils come into being? Even if he says that he can raise a family, how can he be without God, because righteous believers say that nothing happens without him, so why do people go the way of Satan, how many are there in the way of God? It is said that God wants the best for everyone, but why don't people stop him from doing the devil's work? But why Is Satan more powerful than God? No evil guide has come for the devil And if he also breeds, then he is as powerful as Satan's God. And if someone says that the devil cannot increase the lineage, then how did so many devils come into being? Even if he says that he can raise a family, how can he be without God, because righteous believers say that nothing happens without him, so why do people go the way of

Satan, how many are there in the way of God? It is said that God wants the best for everyone, but why don't people stop him from doing the devil's work? But why Is Satan more powerful than God? No evil guide has come from the devil And if he also breeds, then he is as powerful as Satan's God. And if someone says that the devil cannot increase the lineage, then how did so many devils come into being? Even if he says that he can raise a family, how can he be without God, because righteous believers say that nothing happens without him, so why do people go the way of Satan, how many are there in the way of God? It is said that God wants the best for everyone, but why don't people stop him from doing the devil's work? But how did so many devils come into being? Even if he says that he can raise a family, how can he be without God, because righteous believers say that nothing happens without him, so why do people go the way of Satan, how many are there in the way of God? It is said that God wants the best for everyone, but why don't people stop him from doing the devil's work? But how did so many devils come into being? Even if he says that he can raise a family, how can he be without God, because righteous believers say that nothing happens without him, so why do people go the way of Satan, how many are in the way of God? It is said that God wants the best for everyone, but why don't people stop him from doing the devil's work?

3) If action is the only way to get results, then what does God need?

It is said, and also by various religious scholars, that everything is a gift from God If he doesn't do it, even if he does a thousand deeds, it won't work How true is that? Yes, that is not true People generally believe that what God is giving is happening This is definitely wrong Why not, if a person does not do any kind of action will not get results God will not eat If anyone believes this, it must be shown If you don't cook rice, you will be able to eat rice, that is, you will have to work And if people get fruit by doing deeds now, then what is the need to get fruit in heaven, what is the need of God.

4) Why do we need human money to worship God?

It is not uncommon for scholars of various religions and committees of worship to extort money from people. We usually need money for human work, but here it is the opposite God's devotees say it is God's house, or place of worship, or place of worship. In this case, God is so helpless that people need money to worship His devotees. Can't God Himself build a temple for the devotees? So what is the difference between God and ordinary people? Devotees have to work hard to worship, how many people have to be touched, and no one pays. Many times people are in need, yet they are forced to pay tribute under the pressure of society, but why can't God build a temple without hurting people, but he doesn't. In fact, he can't do that Or how he can, He is just a fiction and a human belief He did not show any such magic in the world, nor did he show any proof of the magic that can be heard or the story of how many centuries ago.

5) How many heaven and hell?

According to various religious scriptures, heaven and hell are spoken of in almost every religion. But in Islam, there are eight heavens and seven hells Heaven and hell speak differently in different religions, but they have a division of punishment and peace In Hinduism there are descriptions of the eighty punishments of hell, but hell is one and heaven is one. And in more different religions one is called বলা But if you look at Islam, you can see that knowledge is contradictory, why not Paradise Eight and Hell Seven. That is to say, it is the confusion of God's head, why not the number of sinners on earth. Suppose three percent of one hundred percent worship God and heaven for them But God is less loving, so the number of the heavens should be less, but He has done more, but why. Then many God-fearing people may say, Forgive the sins of sinners and send them to heaven If God forgave many sinners and sent them to heaven, did God see to it that He was righteous? And there are more sinners in the world, but he has reduced the number of hells, so will there be a mountain of huge people or a place there. Where to keep I And if Christianity is a pre-Islamic religion, then there is heaven and hell in Christianity. But the God who sent Judeo-Christian

Islam and it has been sent by different prophets from age to age, but why their heaven is one hell one, again that God said eight heavens and seven hells in Islam, then God is wrong from time to time. And if this is the character of God, then what will be the condition of the devotees? Then what a huge mountain of people will find a place there Where to keep | And if Christianity is a pre-Islamic religion, then there is heaven and hell in Christianity. But the God who sent Judeo-Christian Islam and it has been sent by different prophets from age to age, but why their heaven is one hell one, again that God said eight heavens and seven hells in Islam, then God is wrong from time to time. And if this is the character of God, then what will be the condition of the devotees? Then what a huge mountain of people will find a place there Where to keep | And if Christianity is a pre-Islamic religion, then there is heaven and hell in Christianity. But the God who sent Judeo-Christian Islam and it has been sent by different prophets from age to age, but why their heaven is one hell one, again that God said eight heavens and seven hells in Islam, then God is wrong from time to time. And if this is the character of God, then what will be the condition of the devotees? So does God make mistakes from time to time? And if this is the character of God, then what will be the condition of the devotees? So does God make mistakes from time to time? And if this is the character of God, then what will be the condition of the devotees?

6) Is God Merciful or Compassionate?

Followers of various religions and religious scholars often say that God is merciful and compassionate. But the devotees of God may not know that only man can be merciful Why don't people show kindness to others and show kindness to others, and the word kindness can only be used for man, not for God. The merciful can pity someone and cannot pity someone For example, Karim saved Ram from danger, that is, Karim who had mercy on Ram, this is the work of the merciful, not the merciful. Merciful man means who is not God Then God cannot be merciful in this way, because He is not human So can God be merciful or not? Why can't an entity or an individual see everyone equally, be it God or man? The word merciful means to show kindness to all equally, The word may means all or all In fact, it is evident that the believers in God say that Rama drowned and Shyam survived, so what kindness could Ram and Shyam show? If one is drowned and the other is saved, can God be merciful? River erosion in Samserganj area of Jalangi block under Murshidabad district in September 2020 Hundreds of people lost their homes, land, money, papers, animals and everything else. Many people, even children, old people, cows, goats, etc., have had to leave the world The people there will not see any improvement for the next thirty years What was wrong? One or two can be blamed, so everyone has to be floated in the water, what kind of God The people there shouted "Allah Allah bhagwan bhagwan", bursting their throats, praying in the mosque and crying. Nothing happened with worship in the temple, So what can I say, God is stone, heartless It is said that God loves a man seventy times more than he loves a man, so is there any quality or love of God in it? What was wrong with the baby animals? Where did anyone please Even after this, it can be said that God is merciful Thousands of people came to their side Kni Muhammad Toha Sheikh also discussed various poems about him Even though God is with the believers, where was he hidden that day? Didn't stand next to it God can never be merciful Then what is the quality or love of God in it? What did baby animals do wrong? Where did anyone please Even after this, it can be said that God is merciful Thousands of people came to their side Kni Muhammad Toha Sheikh also discussed various poems about him Even though God is with the believers, where was he hidden that day? Didn't stand next to it God can never be merciful Then what is the quality or love of God in it? What was wrong with the baby animals? Where did anyone please Even after this, it can be said that God is merciful Thousands of people came to their side Kni Muhammad Toha Sheikh also discussed various poems about him Even though God is with the believers, where was he hidden that day? 6 did not stand beside God can never be merciful

7) Is God arbitrary or constitutional?

In general, we all know that arbitrariness is outside the rules, that is, any agreement is bound by the constitution. If any work goes beyond the rules or one's own rights, it is called arbitrariness When God is arbitrary, His greatness is destroyed And how to protect the request of the fans if the rules are Tantric

Defending the recommendation means doing something against one's will That is to do what he himself did not do God will not do anything against His will at the request or recommendation of any individual

8) Does any action or event happen against the will of God?

It is said that nothing happens without God's will, not even the leaf of a tree moves. Especially if something happens due to his reluctance, then where is his greatness. And if everything is according to His will, then what is the fault of the living being.

Farmer Statement

Farmer's statement

I was born in the village. I have been God since I was little

I was a timid person. From the age of seven or eight

I used to go to the mosque regularly. I had nothing to do but study and worship Allah. Life was going very well. Religious life too. I was not very good at reading, but today I have found a place in the court of the world as an established writer. I know that these writers and poets are of no value to some educated people in the village, I don't think they have all become juntas, however, I would not have lacked various studies on Islam. Of course not in any religious school. I used to study Hadith at home. Islamic knowledge is not inferior, but sufficient. Gradually learning, Since I am getting education, I can be called educated. Many may be itchy. I was studying Hadith, Koran, Science, History and Philosophy. I am learning to sort out the hadith by reading various religious books. And that's why people were jealous of me. Because after gaining knowledge, I went against the Hanafi view and started worshiping Allah according to Safi. The people's minds were burning in the fire. People started saying bad things. Began to slander. But not all people know that there is no party, no leader in Islam. Without. People are busy with their respective team leaders. That is why there is no similarity between Muslims in the Muslim world. Conflicts between society, party, country, religion and individual continue all the time. Despite the development of this religion in the modern educated age, there has been no consensus among the minds of the pious, there has been no development of the pious, On the contrary, the decline has increased a thousandfold. But the three of them introduced Islam and Ekjati as closed. They are divided into hundreds of groups and follow different opinions. Islam has thrown religion into the sewers of adultery. And this may be why Islam is being humiliated in the court of the world for some uneducated and uneducated priests and followers of all religions of the world did not hesitate to wear the militant badge, but they did not call Islam militant, said some Muslims. But the list of these activities is not short. They have formed various groups in the name of muhaddiths with various knowledgeable qualities. But the scientists did not go to any team. They are highly knowledgeable personalities, and some dishonest personalities have made a name for themselves by creating groups, but in reality there is no group in Islam. Islam is considered enough for the human race. Anyway, at least I didn't go down without explaining myself first. At least I was right. There was not much of a problem with that, on the way, wherever he went in the field, he used to taunt me by saying Arki, Faraji Faraji. Among them, Namazi Benaji, Bhandalok, the wise, the ignorant, all of them say the same thing, Faraji, or I or against the society. I want to tell them what they mean by society. What is society. Does society have any fixed rules. Not being insulted in the name of society. But no one put me in love and asked me a question with a smile, why I went against another opinion or why I ignored the intellect of all the people in the society. First of all I did not go against any society and opinion. I have changed my mind by selecting the hadith verification and reviewing it wisely, I did not accept any great personality as Imam or leader. But did I go against any law of Islam. Couldn't go. I will look at Islam with respect and devotion till my last death. All the opinions I changed were the words of the Prophet. People used to call me Faraji, but now they don't call me Senami. They don't call me front but call me anti-Islam because I wrote against Islam a few days ago. That, of course, is on Facebook. Of course that is why I will come to the next discussion. First of all, my question is, am I at all anti-Islamic, atheist, infidel, anti-social, hypocritical or a follower of a prophet who seeks correct Islamic law or a Muslim? In answer to this I will say, I am an Islamic or a follower of the Prophet and a Muslim who verifies the correct law. My religion is Islam. Whether he will be recognized by the people of the world or not is their personal matter. If a person has faith in God, Is he an atheist, anti-social, anti-religion worshiper of God as much as he can in religion? Reader's opinion. If there are different personalities in the society with different qualities like unbelievers, usurers, adulterers, adulterers, wrongdoers, religion business, etc., if the people are not anti-social, anti-religion, atheist for the society, can I also say, I am a believer in Allah?

Muslim. But sadly, the above evil people are not known as anti-social, atheist, anti-religion, adulterer, why did I become anti-social, anti-religious in my time. So am I not a Muslim out of love for Islam and devotion to Allah, They are Muslims. But no, I have some faults, so I think I am anti-religion. But what was my fault then. Yes, it was my fault, but I wrote a protest letter to a group of dishonest scholars and tribal chiefs. I was writing the truth. That is what made me engage in anti-social stigma due to the ignorance of some people, but it did not occur to me at all. But what I wrote. Who read what, who understood what. And that's what I meant. What did they understand? No, I wrote it wrong. They had more understanding than I could say. The question will stand in the mind of the reader. You know that I have made a name for myself in the literary circles of Bengal, of course, for your sake. In 2019, Bangla Sahitya Patrika called me a young rebel writer of Bengal with the title of Sahitya Ratna, of course you know. You have read my various digital books in different countries of the world including Bangladesh, Did you get hurt in writing my words. Even though my village does not know about me, today all the writing and literary circles of Bengal know what kind of people NK Mandal is. What I have given to people and what people have given me. Even though the name Dham is with the people of Bengal, it is not in my place, because I am ashamed. The only reason for shame is that I am anti-religious. What were my Facebook posts. Now I will know, I will understand, I will analyze justice. What exactly were the writings

The questions were,

1. "The development of Islam can never be achieved by a broken knee mullah"?

What did you mean by that saying, what did I mean by that? Did you really understand something or not? Didn't you understand the way I wanted to say? Nor did you have the ability to understand correctly, nor did you have that

But the righteous brothers were ready to kill me for saying this But it is not a fierce mood. But did you know that if you hit me, said something and broke down the house, you would still understand something What would be your benefit? Not to meet the anger of your fierce body Judge for yourself what happened But have you ever wondered what the damage is? No, you didn't have time to think like that, because then you are angry with me And when there is anger, nothing is judged and analyzed But do you know what you have lost? First of all, in the eyes of other religions, you are a militant, terrorist, angry person The second is that your religion will make your religion look bad in the eyes of others for your evil deeds (beatings). Thirdly, the village of your society will be infamous Fourth, the writer must be killed and buried, But will there be any work in it. No, this question will be solved Then what is the use of shouting like a fool all over the country? No, you will have dignity among the educated and wise people I know that even though you are educated at the present time, you have been educated to call "Talbya-s" as "Talbassa" So what I really meant is,

"Knee-broken mullah" means half-educated We say in common language equal to the knee, what does it mean I Meaning young, short-sighted, and short or half Did I say wrong? And Mollah does not mean bad things but good and pure words Seventy years ago, Mollah language was used for tribal husbands Mollah is a mixed language, which means Gotrapati, Moral, Samaj Director etc. If the common educated people think that Mollah means scholar, then he is wrong in my sense Scholars are not called mullah anywhere They are called Pandits, Priests, Maulanas, Qaris, Hapez, Muftis. But without understanding what I wanted to say, what I meant, I was overwhelmed If you don't understand whose writing, It was not better for him to know Then either he would say what is good about me But isn't it their fault? Is it not the work of their education or ignorance? Nor did I have any animosity or enmity towards any of the scholars, the people of the society, the leaders of the society. No I said the words aimed at my society. No, I said referring to the most common people in the world and all religions, countries, nations I may have said it in my Islamic language, but that's why I said bad things to someone If I had really written against Islam and the scholars, today I might be under the government of India and Japan. I could have been the owner of a lot of money sitting down. Lots and lots of government and private companies were and still are. I have that power But I love Islam more than my life, I worship it, so I will never do anything against

Islam, Why is there no Muslim blood in my body. I also feel bad when I talk nonsense about Islam, but I am not extremist If necessary, I will explain to him, I will ask him why he is talking nonsense about Islam. So I wanted to say that Islamic society cannot be improved with a semi-educated person. That is, Islamic knowledge is necessary to run the Islamic empire.

My second statement was,

2. "Ninety-eight scholars are liars and religious businessmen in this country"

(Alem is an Arabic language, which means knowledge I this word comes from Alem, which means knowledge)

What I mean is, "this country" means India All the scholars of Islam in India today are telling the truth What is the greed of the three? There is no earning in a wicked way He does not make his stomach fat by collecting in the name of madrasa Students of one madrasa go to another madrasa and do not earn a name there The Hanafi scholars slander the Farajis, and the Faraji scholars slander the Hanafis. How many scholars have been or are being raped in Bangladesh by raping a boy or a girl in a madrasa? How many scholars are eating batapari 6 Those who do not have the same minds as the scholars, what kind of teachers are they? Whose character is absolutely disgusting, even worse than ordinary people No matter how many scholars there are, About ninety-eight percent are busy with their own family How many scholars are correct? Did I have any opposition to the two percent scholars? Then I could say at first that all the scholars are bad and businessmen But I didn't say that, why didn't I say that Because those two percent scholars are beautiful and important personalities for Islam I always respect, trust, love, salute, respectful and obedient to them They are high level personalities They are like diamond inlaid crowns to me Doing business in the name of religion, why don't you protest even if it is a reality? Why don't you take any action against religion traders? In fact, all three of them are scholars The scholar has bought the head He is a scholar, that is, he is a religious scholar, what has happened in that? That is why we have to accept wrong deeds How many people work against the law of Islam? For example, he eats usury, acts illegally, commits adultery with his mother, commits adultery with his wife, He fights with terrorists, forcibly takes bets, even after a divorce in a government court, he gets a halal wife within a day, rapes an old woman, makes bad comments about Islam from front to back, but protests against them. Not judging correctly No. Those who judge whether they are the right person Nor do they have the power to judge No, there is no base in their character In fact, it is not, I feel very poor and weak that's why I But he doesn't know that if he wants to stay in this country, he has to obey the local laws The constitution of this country has given fundamental rights Gave the right to speak Gave individual freedom, yet wise people have to face various problems However, one of my advice came to mind later The difference between ordinary and extraordinary 6 The difference is that out of a hundred people, everyone is extraordinary No, no One in a hundred people is extraordinary, And all people are common That means you are a well-educated person This is not to say that you know the answers to all the questions Or know all the dictionaries And there is something in the dictionary that is one of the same words My esteemed writer Bankimchandra Chattopadhyay said that if a person wants to be a student, a master, a doctor, a barrister, study, but if a person wants to be a writer, he tells him to read and read more. Because if you want to be a writer, you have to read first, but you have to read a lot Because he has knowledge of language and dictionary But I think it is very important to know what one is saying, what one is trying to convey, what kind of dictionary one is saying, what kind of dictionary there is in a word. You know the answers to all the questions Or know all the dictionaries And there is something in the dictionary that is one of the same words My esteemed writer Bankimchandra Chattopadhyay said that if a person wants to be a student, a master, a doctor, a barrister, study, but if a person wants to be a writer, he tells him to read and read more. Because if you want to be a writer, you have to read first, but you have to read a lot Because he has knowledge of language and dictionary But I think it's very important to know what one is saying, what one is trying to convey, what kind of dictionary one is saying, what kind of dictionary there is in a word. You know the answers to all the questions Or know all the dictionaries And there is something in the dictionary that is one of the same words My esteemed writer Bankimchandra Chattopadhyay said that if a person wants to be a student, master, doctor, barrister, study, but if a person wants to be a writer, he has told him to study and read more. Because if you want to be a writer, you have to read first, but you have to read a lot Because he has knowledge of language and vocabulary But I think it's very important to know what one is saying, what one is trying to convey, what kind of dictionary one is saying, what kind of dictionary there is in a word. But you have to read a lot Because he has knowledge of language and vocabulary But I think it's very important to know what one is saying, what one is trying to convey, what kind of dictionary one is saying, what kind of dictionary there is in a word. But you have to read a lot Because he has knowledge of language and dictionary But I think it is very important to know what one is saying, what one is trying to convey, what kind of dictionary one is saying, what kind of dictionary there is in a word.

Thirdly, the question 6 about my name Or do I use Hindu names? Everyone knows my original name, that's why I didn't say anything But their problem is with my name I can't go to paradise with this name The karma of my personal life will take me to paradise or hell I don't think anyone needs anything for that At first they thought my name was NK Mandal i.e. Nishit Kumar Mandal, Nirananda Kumar Mandal meant something to them anyway. But even this has made them look very uneducated and stupid Can anyone say the right thing with a short name? We usually know some short names, such as PM, CM, DM, etc. But how can I say your short name Yes, it is true that my name was given by the Sahitya Mahal of Bengal What is my name? My pseudonym is 6 The name is, Nawaz Karim Mandal 6 So haven't I used the Muslim name non-Muslim? I may not know their names, but it is true that they were in the middle of nowhere. Or I think they used to eat fresh cannabis, because they are mostly drunk. So they misinterpreted I Anyway, there is knowledge, but then it did not come to mind